Letter To Joseph Hume Upon The Mischievous Effects Of Stamp Duties Upon Policies Of Marine Assurance

William Ellis

LETTER

TO

JOSEPH HUME, ESQ. M. P.

UPON THE

MISCHIEVOUS EFFECTS

OF

STAMP DUTIES

UPON

POLICIES

OF

MARINE ASSURANCE.

BY

WILLIAM ELLIS.

London:

Printed by J. Innes, 61, Wells Street, Oxford Street.

1826.

To Joseph Hume, Esq. M. P.

SIR,

      IN pursuance of the promise which I made some days ago, I now propose to address you a few lines on the subject of the existing stamp duties upon policies of marine assurance. The duties are as follow:—

For every £100 insured on a voyage in the coasting trade of the United Kingdom, where the premium does not exceed 20s per cent. 1s 3d

    Where it does exceed 20s per cent. 2s 6d

For every £100 insured to or from any colonial or foreign part, where the premium does not exceed 20s per cent. 2s 6d

    Where it does exceed 20s per cent. 5s

For every £100 insured on ships for time (no ship can be insured for time on one stamp, for a period exceeding 12 months) 5s

4

With regard to the stamp on coasting voyages, nobody can avoid seeing that it acts as a direct discouragement to shipping. On valuable merchandize, more especially, the advantage of water as compared with land carriage is considerably diminished by such a duty. When a merchant has goods to transmit from one part of the kingdom to another, he naturally calculates what the cost of carriage is likely to be by every species of conveyance, and selects that which is cheapest. It should be the care of every legislator, in raising a revenue, not to extract more from the industry of the people than can possibly find its way into the exchequer. A tax, the effect of which is to divert capital from one channel into another, must always be an unwise tax, because the community are not only deprived of that which is needed to meet the expenses of government, but are made to suffer in addition that loss which cannot fail to attend the diversion of capital from the more to the less profitable employment.

Suppose a merchant has two parcels of goods worth £20,000 each, to send from London to Liverpool, one of great bulk and the other of small bulk. Suppose the charges of conveyance upon the bulky goods, before any stamp duty was imposed, were £400 by canal, and £200

5

by sea. After the duty was imposed, the charges by sea would be increased to £212. 10s. The merchant would still continue to send his bulky goods by sea; and the consumers at Liverpool would pay for this additional charge in an increased price. So far the tax would not take more from the consumers than it would produce to the exchequer. But how would the case be with the goods of small bulk? Suppose, before the tax was imposed, the expenses of conveyance upon them were £150 by canal, and £145 by sea. After the tax was imposed, the charges by sea would be increased to £157. 10s. The merchant, accordingly, after the tax was imposed, would send his goods of small bulk by canal. The operation of the tax, therefore, upon the two parcels of goods would be to produce £12. 10s to the exchequer, and to decrease the enjoyments of the community to the extent of £17. 10s. I am ready to admit that the tax, although impolitic, is small, and that consequently the mischiefs which flow from it must be small likewise. But there is no reason why the smallest mischiefs should not be remedied, especially when the remedy can be applied without difficulty or inconvenience. That the tax is wrong in principle, cannot be denied. Indeed it might be shown, that were the tax sufficiently enlarged, (assuming that parties could

6

be *forced* to insure their property) the whole coasting trade of Great Britain would be annihilated.

If the stamp duties upon the coasting trade are wrong in principle, those on the foreign trade are still more so. It is now well known, that the foundation of all commerce is, *the difference of relative facility in the production of certain commodities.* England imports wine from France, because, after paying all the charges of transport, she can procure it on cheaper terms than she could produce it herself. In like manner, France imports hardware from England for the same reason. Every thing which increases the charges of conveyance, tends to diminish foreign commerce. There are many imported commodities, which, after the expenses of transport are paid, cost a trifle less than they would have cost had they been produced in this country. There are many exported commodities, which, after the same expenses are paid, can be sold a trifle cheaper than they can be produced abroad. It is perfectly clear that every thing which adds to the charges of transport tends to destroy all trade in commodities of this description. A tax, therefore, which swells these charges, takes more from the subject than it produces to the exchequer. The manner in which this effect is produced, is the same as I have described above; and repetition would be tedious.

But this is not the only mischief of a tax upon the insurance of property *in transitû* to and from foreign ports. No foreigners are concerned in the home trade; and as merchants prefer having their securities upon the spot, the insurances connected with that trade are effected in this country, and the stamp is submitted to. In the foreign trade, however, one of the parties engaged, the consigner, or consignee, is generally a foreigner. The chances, therefore, are that insurances upon the property at stake will be effected where they can be done upon the most moderate terms. As there is no reason why the rate of insurance should be higher at Hamburgh, Paris, or New York, than at London, if at this latter port the property to be insured is subjected to a heavy charge in addition, the owners of such property will, unless prevented by other circumstances, order their insurances *not* to be effected at London. General reasoning, then, clearly leads to the conclusion, that a country, situated as England is, with a heavy duty upon policies of marine assurance, while there is no duty in foreign countries, or at most but a nominal one, must inevitably lose a large portion of her insurance business ; and this conclusion is fully confirmed by practical experience. There is hardly a merchant in this country, connected with foreign parts, who could not bring forward some instance of a correspondent's withholding orders of insurance on account of our stamp duties. It is notorious that France, Germany, and America, at present take from us a large portion of our insurance business. Whereas, there can be no doubt, that were our stamp duties repealed, were this country placed upon an equal footing with her neighbours, her immense capital and undoubted security would obtain for her a decided preference. As an example of the proportion which the stamp bears to the premium of insurance, it may be stated, that the premium to and from Liverpool and the United States, during the summer months, seldom exceeds 20s per cent : the stamp is 2s 6d per cent. During the winter months, the premium varies from 25s to 40s per cent : the stamp is 5s per cent. During the greater part of the year, to and from the Continent, the premium is from 5s to 15s per cent. while the stamp is 2s 6d per cent ! I need not stop to draw inferences from these facts : they speak for themselves.

It must be borne in mind, that the insurance business,

like every other business, must produce to those employed in it, after a remuneration for their risk, the ordinary profits of stock. And, accordingly, the national income must be diminished by every regulation the effect of which is to drive this business out of the country. The destruction of any part of the national income, makes the expences of the state fall heavier upon the remainder. But the evils which flow from this source are so well known, that the mere allusion to them is sufficient.

If the operation of this tax, as it affects the British ship-owner, be considered, nothing will be found to reconcile us to the evils which I have pointed out. It may be assumed, that British ships will, in most cases, be insured in this country, and that foreign ships will be insured abroad. The stamp duty upon policies of assurance on ships may be computed at $\frac{1}{2}$ per cent. per annum upon their value. In some cases it will exceed, in others it will fall short of this amount. But from what I can collect, $\frac{1}{2}$ per cent. per annum upon the value of the ship is a low estimate of what the ship-owner contributes to the policy stamp. This $\frac{1}{2}$ per cent, as far as it can be supposed to operate, is a premium upon the employment of foreign in preference to British shipping.

It may be said, however, allowing the stamp upon policies of marine assurance to be an impolitic tax, it produces £240,000 per annum to the exchequer. And if every body is to be listened to, we shall hear that all taxes are impolitic. Some will grumble at one tax—some at another. This unfortunately is true, and the best taxes are not those which have excited the least grumbling. But because taxes must be levied, there is no reason why they should not be levied with the least possible detriment and inconvenience to the community. And, I think, I have shewn satisfactorily certain specific mischiefs which are inseparably attached to policy stamps. As to the £240,000 which the policy stamps produce to the exchequer, if the community can afford to pay that sum in one shape, they can afford to pay it in another. There can be no necessity for me to enter into a lengthened argument to prove that the £240,000 which the policy stamps produce is paid by the consumers of the goods which are insured upon those stamps. Any body who is likely to interest himself about a question of this description, will be too enlightened to be deceived by assertions to the contrary. If, then, the £240,000 be paid by the consumers of goods, why should not this sum be levied directly upon the goods themselves? Why should not all the evils which I have pointed out be got rid of? Why should not the capitalists of this country be allowed to compete with their neighbours on fair terms in the insurance business? Why should the British ship-owner be subjected to unnecessary disadvantages? Why should not the industry of this country be allowed to flow into those channels in which the greatest quantity of wealth will be secured to the community?

There are two modes in which the tax upon policies might be, with great facility, transferred to the goods :— either by raising a per centage upon the customs duties which are now levied, or by imposing an additional duty upon particular commodities.

The first of these modes would, I conceive, be the best of the two. If it were adopted, as the customs of this country yield about £10,000,000, a rate of 2½ per cent. (to be called a commutation for the tax upon policies) would produce £250,000.

As an example of the method of executing the commutation according to the second of these plans, I will suppose the commodities upon which it was determined that the £240,000 should be levied, were Sugar, Coffee, and Tallow. The home consumption of these commodities is about 2,500,000 cwt. of sugar, 4,000,000 lbs. of coffee, and 600,000 cwt. of tallow. A tax of 6d per cwt. on the first article, of 6d per lb. on the second, and of 2s 6d per cwt. on the last, would together produce upwards of £250,000.

Another advantage which is to be gained by a transfer of the duty from the policy to the goods, is the diminution of expense. The charges for printing and distributing the policies, and for examining claims, and making allowances upon spoiled stamps, cannot, I should think, be far short of £10,000 per annum, a sum by no means so small as to be beneath the notice of a wise administration.

It must occur to every body, that peculiar facilities are presented for the evasion of this tax. The consequences of such facilities are always pernicious. The tendency of them is to demoralize, to obscure the limits between right and wrong. Where the laws are such that the temptation to disobey them is strong, there will crime infallibly be generated. A tax upon insurance is, moreover, a tax upon forethought; it causes imprudence to assume a lucrative appearance. This observation applies, perhaps, with still greater force to the stamp-duty upon fire assurance than it does to that on marine assurance. The object of every enlightened legislator should be, if possible, to caution the heedless, and to attach the highest advantages to the exercise of discretion. By such means is the happiness of communities to be established.

When I reflect upon the extensive and important improvements which have of late years been introduced into our commercial regulations, and upon the sound principles which have so frequently been put forward, I am persuaded that no means will be despised by which any good, however trifling, may be produced. While the mind is occupied with vast and striking objects, others less obtrusive easily escape the attention. For this reason I am not surprized that his Majesty's ministers should have omitted to notice the impolicy of the existing stamp duty upon marine assurances. If their attention is once directed to the few suggestions which I have thrown together, I feel little doubt that the repeal of this obnoxious tax will speedily follow. In the expectation of this desirable event,

I remain, Sir,

Your most obedient servant,

WILLIAM ELLIS.

J. Innes, Printer, 61, Wells-st. Oxford-st. London.